Midnight Stroll

poems by

Steve Cushman

Finishing Line Press
Georgetown, Kentucky

Midnight Stroll

Copyright © 2016 by Steve Cushman
ISBN 978-1-944251-16-1 First Edition
All rights reserved under International and Pan-American Copyright Conventions. No part of this book may be reproduced in any manner whatsoever without written permission from the publisher, except in the case of brief quotations embodied in critical articles and reviews.

ACKNOWLEDGMENTS

Aries: Silent Time
Bellevue Literary Review: Out Back, Behind the Hospital
Broad River Review: Owls
Flying South: Spring
Friendly Naturalist: Red-headed Woodpecker
Harmony: Hospital Hopscotch & After Leaving My Mother at the Hospital
Iodine Poetry Journal: Help Desk, My Mother's Bologna Sandwich & Plums
Kakalak: What She Sees & Secrets
Main Street Rag: Grandfather
O Henry: At The Playground & Sophomore Biology
100 Word Story: Morning Light
Pinestraw: My Father's Golf Clubs
Prose Poem: Midnight Stroll & Junior
Salt: The Truth About Birds and Marriage
Taking Flight: Moon
Waccamaw: Tree Stump

Editor: Christen Kincaid

Cover Art: Matthew Johnson, "Tyres"

Author Photo: Jan G. Hensley

Cover Design: Elizabeth Maines

Printed in the USA on acid-free paper.
Order online: www.finishinglinepress.com
also available on amazon.com

Author inquiries and mail orders:
Finishing Line Press
P. O. Box 1626
Georgetown, Kentucky 40324
U. S. A.

Table of Contents

Midnight Stroll 1
Tree Stump 2
Grandfather 3
Out Back, Behind the Hospital 4
At The Playground 5
Hospital Hopscotch 6
Silent Time 7
I'm True 8
The Truth About Birds and Marriage 9
Junior 10
What She Sees 11
Sophomore Biology 12
After Leaving My Mother at the Hospital 13
Spring 14
Red-headed Woodpecker 15
When They Tell Me 16
My Mother's Bologna Sandwich 17
Help Desk 18
Secrets 19
Plums 20
Moon 21
Morning Light 22
Playing Pool 23
My Father's Golf Clubs 24
Owls 25

For my Mother and Father, Joyce and Steve

Midnight Stroll

She would wait until my father was asleep,
then pluck me from my bed, lead me around
the neighborhood, smelling of wine and cigarettes.
She would tell me about the people who lived in
the houses we passed, which ones were cheating on
their spouses, which ones came home for lunch every day.
She would tell me about my father too, how he had been a great
potter once but he'd given it up to pay the rent. I didn't
know if anything she said was true, or if it even mattered.
She was my mother, it was after midnight, I was seven years old,
and together we walked the dark night, hand in hand,
while all around us the world slept.

Tree Stump

My wife and I dug into
the hard ground to remove
the dead dogwood
while my neighbor loaded
his guitar into his new car
waved to us in his shades and
flip flops, said he had a gig to play,
and how I wished I had a gig to play,
but there was no gig for me to play,
so on that Saturday in May
we kept digging,
past dirt, past orange clay,
past root and worm,
past little yellow plastic army figures,
and when it was almost dark and my back was tired
and the only thing I could think of
were those cold beers waiting for me
my shovel hit something solid
and I dug it out, dug out this
black rock that I thought might
be shale and my wife laughed
and said it was probably coal and I held
it up to what was left of the sun
and the rock was covered in dirt so I threw it
on the ground to crack it to get to its core
to see what was inside and in there
it was shiny and black with flakes of silver
and I lifted the rock to my nose and smelled it
and it smelled like nothing and it smelled like earth
and every perfect thing we hide away
so I slid it in my pocket and went back
to work to get this stump out of the ground
to try and get to the heart of this thing.

Grandfather

And later, I visited him
at the trailer park he owned
in Pinellas Park, Florida and together
we travelled by golf cart down
Stevie Lane and *Kimberly Way*
roads he'd named after my sister and me
and we passed a pony and an alligator
and we passed other golf carts, three-wheeled bicycles
propelled forward by neighbors whose names he'd forgotten
and when we reached the end,
there in his covered driveway
he asked me to go inside for some water.
When I returned, he was slumped
over the steering wheel
his forehead pressed against
his white driving gloves
and before I said a word, before I touched him
I thought of the man he used to be
back when he was still the King of Wareham
and we drove the streets of that Massachusetts town
in his baby blue convertible Cadillac
back when I was his sidekick, his grandson,
the likely heir to his trailer park dynasty.

Out Back, Behind the Hospital

We shared cigarettes and jokes
talked about anything except
what we'd seen, the baby we'd X-rayed,
his bruises, his broken arm,
the way he'd opened his mouth to cry
but no sound came, his tears, his eyes wide
but still he didn't make a sound.
At 2 months old, he'd already learned
the importance of silence, so out back
behind the hospital, Fred and I talked
about the Super Bowl, where we'd
like to go skiing, our plans for the weekend,
anything but what we'd seen yet had no words for.

At The Playground

My four year old doesn't play
with other kids; he lives in his
imagination throws his hands
in the air, fingers writing the sky
like tiny birds and when the other
children turn and stare, I want
to tell him to stop doing that
to just ride down the damn slide, swing
on the swings, like everyone else
but he is only being himself,
someone I am still not comfortable with.

Hospital Hopscotch

No one knows where it came from,
a hopscotch board on a sidewalk,
leading into the children's hospital,
but as quick as it appeared, so did
the children, laughing and hopping,
in their hospital gowns and isolation masks,
holding onto their IV poles for balance
as they count the boxes and hop, hop
all the way from one to ten and back again.

Silent Time

Having lunch with my son in the elementary school cafeteria
I am struck by the volume of children. Their willingness to talk
louder and louder, over one another. My son is telling me about
his spelling test, about how he thinks he did pretty well.

But then the piano starts, indicating silent time, a five minute
reprieve from the noise and chatter of children's voices,
their lives and concerns as important to them as their parents'
own worries. For a few minutes they go back to their peanut
butter and jelly sandwiches, their crackers and cheese sticks,
100-calorie snack packs of cookies and chips.

They seem to know when silent time is coming to an end because
from nowhere I hear the first low rumble and then the piano has
stopped and the chorus of a hundred young voices is calling out,
each child singing its own song and yet together it sounds
as beautiful as anything I've ever heard.

I'm True

my six years old says,
meaning I'm telling the truth.

I correct him in the way fathers
are supposed to: *you should
really say I'm telling the truth.*

But he shakes his head, folds
arms tight across his chest and says,
no Dad, I'm true, really, I'm true.

I start to correct him again, then
catch myself, say, *yes, I know
Trevor, you are true.*

The Truth About Birds and Marriage

On my friend's wedding day,
a pair of waxwings flew into his bay window.
We were at his house, on the side of the mountain,
listening to the preacher explain the importance
of marriage and vows when we heard the thud and turned.
The bride's mother was a vet and she said
to put the birds in a brown paper bag.
She said they were probably only stunned and needed
the darkness and quiet to recover. And eventually,
as we drank and danced, there was a rustling in the bag,
so we opened it and the birds flew up and away and we cheered.

Years later, when my friend and his wife
were in the middle of a divorce a few of our friends
said those birds were a bad omen. But I've been married
long enough now to know it wasn't a pair of birds
crashing into the window that doomed them.
It's usually nothing as dramatic as that
but more the slow winding down of a marriage,
the way it can be chipped away at day after day
and whether or not it's going to last has about as much
to do with birds crashing into windows as it does plain dumb luck.

Junior

To be named after your father
is supposed to be an honor,
and it can feel like it
when you follow him into the bar
and the other men pat him, and you,
on the back, say *about damn time you got here, Steve*.
But what about when you're at his funeral
and the preacher says your name over and over
as he talks about your dead father
and you can't help but feel like it is you,
or a piece of you, they are lowering into the ground forever?

What She Sees

When she was little,
she would climb the oak tree
in her backyard, sit tight against the branches
and watch the world of her family.
She'd watch her sister kiss boys
on the back porch, watch their hands
disappear into her sister's shirt and shorts
the way she'd grabbed their forearms
as if she wanted them to stop
and the girl watched her father practice
his golf swing in the backyard
the way he'd bring his gloved hand
to his eyes as if watching an imaginary
ball coast off into the distance
and she watched her mother
sit on the porch, smoking a cigarette
and whispering into her cell phone,
the way she would laugh, then look
around, as if happiness was something
she needed to hide.

Sophomore Biology

dissecting frogs and what I wanted
was to see the inside of a thing
how its heart kept beating when
all around there was heartbreak,
Dina saying we should be friends now
Dad saying he was going to move out for a bit
and there lay the frog, flayed open, white,
no blood, but of course, this was
something without a beating heart
because those we don't get to see
and all we can do is imagine
the way they squeeze and beat and open
and close and there is Mr. Moore
at the front of the class
talking kidney, talking liver, lungs, all these organs
that meant nothing to me when all I ever wanted
was to get to the heart of things.

After Leaving My Mother at the Hospital

When the light turned green
I didn't press the gas pedal
but stared forward
thinking of my mother
lighting cigarette after cigarette
making me grilled bologna and cheese
sandwiches and the ashtrays
always full, the cups of coffee she drank
those small white cups with her lipstick stains
and I thought about leaving her there in the hospital,
of the doctor's words which meant nothing
to me and what I wanted was to talk to my mother
to tell her I'd be coming over later
with a pepperoni pizza
but I could no longer do this,
so when the drivers behind me
started honking, I threw my keys
into the grassy median and held tight
to the steering wheel, trying to figure out
how to navigate this new world
one where when I called my mother
she would not be there to answer.

Spring

She'd like an apple this morning
perhaps not first thing—there is coffee
and toast and maybe even a hard boiled egg
but after her breakfast and walking the dog
and getting the kids ready for school
she'd like to come home and sit on the white
Wicker chair beside the window and eat a Fuji apple,
watch the birds at the feeder, her cat chasing
the catkins, floating, flying through the light April air.

Red-headed Woodpecker

It's February and the Red-headed woodpecker
is pecking away at the side of my shed.
Perhaps I should scare him off
or replace the wood there, because
eventually he will carve a hole so big
the shed will leak and the hole will grow
and the structure will crumble.
But it's a woodpecker with a bright red head
and its body is round and lean and for
the chance to watch it do its dirty work
I'll gladly pay the cost of a new shed.

When They Tell Me

I know it's true
have always known
his lack of caring for others
the spinning and hands flying
the stemming and figure eights
so when they tell me,
all those people gathered
in a room, I'm not surprised
because I'd known it all along
but had hoped I was wrong.

My Mother's Bologna Sandwich

I can still see her standing at the stove
a cigarette between her thin lips, a spatula
ready to flip the sandwich, the room filling with steam
and smoke, the cheese on top,
another slice of buttered Wonder bread
and like magic the sandwich is in front of me
cut at an angle. *Here Mom*, I say, *have
a bite* and she lifts her hand, her cigarette,
as if that was all she ever needed. But I insist
and her bite is small and mouse-like when all
I ever wanted was to give her the whole damn thing.

Help Desk

I'm working the IT help desk
when a nurse at the Woman's Hospital
calls and tells me her boyfriend
broke up with her, so I say
is your computer working?
Are you able to complete
your patient documentation?
She says *six months and he dumps*
me a week before Christmas.
But your computer, ma'am,
is it working okay? She says
but what I am going to tell my mother
she loved him more than she loved me.
What I should say is you've
called the wrong number
and gently hang up the phone,
but I don't. Instead, I ask
his name and she says *Ray*
and I lean back in my chair,
close my eyes and listen even though
I know I probably won't be able to help her.

Secrets

Come and tell me your secrets
she says, *tell me what*
you are most ashamed of,
so I tell her about you,
your long black hair, your
blue sheets lifted over our heads
brown socks and purple underwear
I tell her about apple butter and walnut bread
and your apartment, that place I escaped
to all those months ago, about how you brought
me back to life and then later I refused your calls
about the day you appeared at my home
and I pretended I didn't even know you.

Plums

My wife and I are throwing
plums at each other. They
are wild plums, no bigger than
a grape, from a tree in our backyard.
At first, it's for fun, but then
she hits me in the throat and it
stings so I throw harder, aim for her
head and when I hit her left ear
she cries out and I run toward her
ashamed and afraid of what I've done
but as I reach her she releases another
handful, hits me in the forehead, the eye,
and I fall to the ground, grab my eye
hear her laugh as the back door
slams shut, leaving me on the ground
wounded and laughing, unable to see,
but already plotting my revenge.

Moon

So let's say
you are driving alone
and thinking
of nothing more than
staying between the lines
and when you crest the hill
see the huge white moon
sitting there as if it had been
waiting for you, and you alone,
out here on a road where there
is not another living soul
for miles and miles.

Morning Light

In the dark morning kitchen
pouring myself a cup of coffee
I hear her voice, the quiet tired hello.
I turn to the table and at first
all I see is a shape, but eventually
she comes in to focus, elbows
on the table, tea mug against
her right cheek, the glow
of the streetlight above her head.

How could I have walked by
and not seen this woman whom
I've spent more than half my life with?
I tell myself it is the darkness,
the lack of sleep and caffeine
but even I don't believe that.

Playing Pool

After my parent's divorce, my father kept a pool table
in the living room of the house he rented. One night,

I climbed out of bed, crept down the hall
and watched him in his baggy white Jockeys

sink ten, twenty, thirty balls with ease.
I wondered why my mother couldn't see this

how she could kick him out. I was only fourteen
young and dumb enough to believe possessing

a certain skill was enough to make people love you.

My Father's Golf Clubs

My father's golf clubs are tucked away
in my attic, beside the old paint cans
and beach chairs and suitcases.
He used these clubs on the day he died
playing golf, almost twenty years ago now.
After his death, my stepmother gave the clubs
to my uncle, who years later gave them to me.
And then when my wife and I moved into our home
a decade ago I set them in a corner of the attic.

A couple times a year, always while searching
for something else, I will spot the golf clubs.
May even pull out his rust-specked putter
or the 7-Wood with the cracked rubber grip,
squeeze it in my hands and imagine him playing
his final round. I wonder if he played well that day,
if he was under or over par. These are the sorts of things
you don't think about until later, much later.

Owls

For the third night in a row we gather
at my neighbor's to watch the owls roost.
There are six of us. We stretch out in
our lawn chairs, drink beer or wine and
look up at the hole in the tall oak and wait
for the male to arrive. When he does, we sigh
as he starts his low and steady whoo, whoo,
calling for her. We watch, we wait and when she
does not come we slowly, one by one, stand
and walk back to our houses. An hour later,
I look outside and see my neighbor--an avid birdwatcher
and recent widow--still standing in her backyard.
I walk over and say Barbara, and she shakes her head
and begins to cry, so I hug her, and she says
*how could sh*e and I say *it's just the way things are*
and she says *you don't know what the hell you're talking
about* and I think she's right, holding her, waiting,
willing that damn bird to get here and show her face.

Steve Cushman earned an undergraduate degree at the University of Central Florida, then an M.A. from Hollins University and his M.F.A. in Creative Writing from the University of North Carolina at Greensboro. His debut novel, *Portisville*, was the winner of the 2004 Novello Literary Award. He has published a second novel, *Heart With Joy*, as well as the short story collection, *Fracture City*, and poetry chapbook, *Hospital Work*.

For the past twenty years, Steve has worked as an X-ray Technologist and is currently employed at Moses Cone Memorial Hospital. He lives in Greensboro, North Carolina with his wife and son. More information on Steve's writing can be found at www.stevecushman.net

www.ingramcontent.com/pod-product-compliance
Lightning Source LLC
Chambersburg PA
CBHW051706040426
42446CB00009B/1324